Dr. Rette

Thank you

May you be blessed

Read the Poems
Read Book

Zonah

From The Heart Of A Poet

by

John Simmons, Jr.

authorHOUSE®

AuthorHouse™
1663 Liberty Drive, Suite 200
Bloomington, IN 47403
www.authorhouse.com
Phone: 1-800-839-8640

First published by AuthorHouse 10/16/2007

ISBN: 978-1-4259-7875-4 (sc)

Library of Congress Control Number: 9781425978754

Printed in the United States of America
Bloomington, Indiana

This book is printed on acid-free paper.

Acknowledgments

I would like to thank God for giving me the courage to embrace my calling and for leading me to walk into my purpose in life. Through this I have learned to embrace the words meekness, goodness, gentleness, faith, love, joy, peace, longsuffering and temperance.

I would also like to thank my darling wife Connie, who I truly love with all my heart. Thank you for all the encouraging words you gave me when I felt down and for being there all the times I hurt inside. To my daughters Nasya and Alanah I love you both and thank you for your smiles and warm hugs. My son John and stepson Martel, thanks for the energy, I truly couldn't have kept up if it weren't for you two setting the pace. Thanks to my mother Virginia Jack-Jacox who has always been an inspiration to me and always has an open ear, always. Thanks to my Pastor and Uncle, John White Sr. for the fatherly words of wisdom. Sheryl Posley, I couldn't have even begun without you.

Stephanie Whittington and Richard Franklin, I thank you for your prayers and support through difficult times. My best friend Willis Cable, you know me inside and out, peace my brother. To Benjamin my brother thanks for the encouragement. Thanks to all my other siblings as well. A special thanks to my manager "RJ", who gave me many words of wisdom and guidance with my acts, performances and also this book. I would finally like to thank everyone who has inspired or encouraged me in any way with this book that I have not mentioned.

God bless you all.

Foreword

It is an honor to share in this historical moment with my son, John Simmons. We are excited about what is happening. He has stepped out into a new dimension, a vast frontier for the specially talented folk. It is a bold step which speaks for itself saying, "I am here and this is what I have to say." So much of John's talent has been hidden for so long. This book took a while for he lived it and then wrote it from his own experiences. It is about love, joy, pain, disappointments, as well as humor splashed throughout with the other inspiring passages. John's heart has been prepared to share.

This book "From The Heart Of A Poet" will pull you into time, the past, the present, and the future. You can be healed from your own soul's crises.

Growing up, John was quiet, always the observer, the thinker; he now has a lot to say. Listen to him. If you are ever in the area of Rockford Illinois, join him with his poet's night out and hear him in person. When visiting there, I find it awesome.

John's poetry has a fresh new fragrance that lightens the air, bringing a new song.

You'll know that life is always worth living and there are many benefits in it. I know you will enjoy this book!

Virginia Jack

Author of "The Blaze And The Balm"

Introduction

I first fell in love with poetry when I was in the seventh grade. I lived in Hammond Indiana and attended a private school in Gary Indiana because my mother was very strict about my education and always wanted the best for my siblings and I. I remember my English teacher just like it was yesterday. Her name was Sister Fitzpatrick. She gave the whole seventh and eighth grade class an enormous assignment that would also double as our final exam. We were studying poetry and famous poets both past and present. We were each assigned a five to six page poem that we had to recite from memory within a thirty day window. I tried a memory technique that required me to recite and record the poem using a tape recorder. I purchased a pair of headphones and listened to my recording while I slept at night. I practiced over and over, night after night for the whole month and I was amazed at how much I had started to remember. Poetry all of a sudden had become exciting to me, it was a challenge. I was never so proud the day I stood before my peers and recited that five page poem.

It gave me a since of pride and accomplishment and I not only wanted to know more, I wanted to do more. After the buzz of successfully completing the task wore off, I just couldn't get rid of the passion that I had developed inside me. Soon I began to read and write more poetry every chance I got. Ever since that moment I never lost the love and respect I had gained for such a beautiful way to express creativity. This is the same expression I have shared with you in this book, as was felt the day I first feel in love with poetry. One amazing fact about this is that I fell in love with poetry before I even started liking girls. I attribute that to my uncanny ability to be able to express myself with words that come straight from my heart. Thus, my love to write, thank you.

Table of Contents

Love & Emotional

Humorous Jazzy Personal & Other

Inspirational

&

Encouragement

Poetry is a deep root that allows words to travel straight from the heart to the mind and from the mind to the mouth. Poetry allows the mind to travel free on the autobahn of thoughts. The true power that poetry holds remains a mystery, but some would swear by her. The tongue itself is so powerful that the Holy Bible even says that the power of life and death is in the tongue. Your words do carry weight and they do have power.

I like to subtitle this chapter as being called "The Mentor", because everyone should have a mentor involved in their lives in some way.

A mentor is someone that can help keep you on track and who can help guide you through and around difficult, trying, indecisive and tough times in life, business and even family. No matter what trials you have been through in your past or even might go through in your future, whether business or personal. This chapter will help give you the inspiration and encouragement that is needed in order to stand up and go the distance.

God's word promises us that we do win in the end.

The Power Within

I have power deep down on the inside of me
I have the power to conquer
Power to overcome
Power to never give up
Power to win
Power to will and to do
Power to speak to a mountain and watch it move

I have power deep down on the inside of me
I have to power to bloom and then blossom
Power to get wealth
Power to give to the people
Power to help others
Power to volunteer
Power to open closed doors and bring new life to a
Dying people

I have power deep down on the inside of me
I have the power to prevail in a losing situation
Power to produce
Power to succeed

Power to try again and again
Power to say no
Power to speak a spoken word into my life
And live

I have power deep down on the inside of me
I have the power to understand
Power to endure
Power to think
Power to comprehend
Power to hope
Power to create
Power to give birth to visions and dreams

I have power deep down on the inside of me
That at any moment I can tap into
This power that I have came not on its own
God who is the giver of every good and
Perfect gift
Has put within every man the ultimate power

I have the power to choose

Daily Choice

Sorrow only last as long as it's invited
The breaking of day usually brings a chance
To leave the past behind
If you continue to look at the past
And if sorrow continues to rule your day
Then, you will never really have
A brighter day
A lighter day
A smilier day
A cooler day
A fuller day
A lovelier day
A kinder day and
Not even a happier day
In fact
You may not even see a day at all
So don't let sorrow rule your day
Sorrow only last
As long as
It's invited

Victory

Don't give up
No, No, No,
Don't give in
If you could only see who really wins in the end
Don't give up
No, No, No
Don't give in
Keep your fire burning like the sound of a
Mighty roaring wind
Don't give up
No, No, No
Don't give in
Your yesterday is gone away, you've come too far to
Turn away and victory is at hand
Don't give up
No, No, No
Don't give in
For as long as you have beat of heart
It doesn't matter what storms you weather
If you will just keep your head together and have
Faith you will soon understand
We all win in the end

Decisions

If the future of the world were in your hands
Tell me
What would you do?
If you could go back in time and began again
Would you instead invade Iran?
If all the eyes in the world looked steadfast
Upon you
Could you glare back at them, one by one and
Explain the whys, the how's and the dos of the
Decisions you make
Or would you just fake it and
Barely try to make it?
When a child cries, who answers their call?
When they ask why, why and why again
Do you just send them away again and again?
Answers are not found in the things you allow
But in the decisions you make
It is there that you can create the things that will
Bring about a change in our world
Just take a look around you

And know that with everything you do
Somebody is watching you and recording
Everything you do
If you really want to decide to do something
Great, then
Choose to help somebody less fortunate than
Yourself everyday in some way
Don't worry about the could've, would've and
The should've that have long pasted you by
But dwell on this;
If the future of the world were in your hands
If you could go back in time and began again
Or if all the eyes in the world looked steadfast
Upon you
Would you still remember the place
Where you once stood?
Only you can
Decide

Effort to Smile

Would you or could you
Have you ever or would you never
Just walk by me with a
Tear in your eye
Could I or would I
Have I ever or would I never
Just stand by and watch the tear
Cross your quivered smile
Only to reach the place where
My feet do meet
Tell me how, tell me now
What must be done to chase away
That runt-of-a-bum
Oh, you have never looked so good
When leaving him behind
Why not now
For how heavy he is to your
Soft brown cheeks
Let's rid him together
Make him run away forever
Then you can say

I have never nor would I ever
Allow that runt of a bum
To pull at my cheeks
A second time around
I realize that sometimes it takes
Two to make a smile
And only one to make a bum
So I choose to help you
Smile
(So smile already will ya!)

Say It

To say YES

        Is to believe that there is always
        Going to be another chance
        At everything

To say YES

        Is to admit to know something
        But don't necessarily know where to
        Find it

To say YES

        Is to understand that everything
        Will, go forward

To say YES

        Is to grant, a wishers wish

To say YES

        Is to agree with everything
        And to deny nothing

To say YES

        Is to agree to have
        Unlimited stresses

Say NO instead

To say NO

> Is to believe that there is always
> Going to be another chance
> Only, if you never give up

To say NO

> Is to deny knowing everything
> Except where to find it

To say NO

> Is to understand that
> Only what you will
> Go forward

To say NO

> Is to never grant a wishers wish
> But always grant a wishers need

To say NO

> Is to denounce everything
> And to agree with nothing

To say NO

> Is to have unlimited peace
> That everyone
> Will soon
> Stop asking

A New Beginning

I'm free
Free to express what I really want to express
I'm free
Free to will that which I would will
I'm free
Free not only in body, but free in the mind
I'm free
Free to walk the paths
That once held forbidden steps
I'm free
Free to smell the
Fragrance of the wind after the rain
Free to fly high in the uncharted parts of the sky
Free to swim in the waters that run deep
To be free is to be boundless without boundaries
If you want to be something you're not
Or if you're simply searching for something
That you don't have
Remember first, that
Your neighbors' prize isn't priced for coveting

If you really want to be and
Remain free
Then one must first learn
To listen without distractions
Walk without the help of others and finally
One must learn to forgive
More than just the faults of others
This will be the beginnings of the rest of your
Free life
So now,
Fly away little eagle

Live On

In looking behind we have all found ways to
Look ahead
Though some through tragedy and some
Through much pain
The fact remains; there is so much to gain
If we but listen to what our hearts have to say
If we would but follow the paths that were
Already paved
How much suffering would now be peace?
How much pain would now be gain?
How much poverty would now be prosperity?
Be encouraged and stand up my child
Look to the hills from whence cometh your help
It is not of this earth that we must put our trust
It is not of this land, that we must make our stand
It is not in the air, to which throne we are heir
Be encouraged and stand up my child
Dead is only dead in the grave
For as long as you breathe
As long as you have spirit

As long as you have beat of heart and
As long as you have the omnipotent one
Dead is only dead in the grave
Your past might be dead
But your future is yet alive
So live, live, live on today
Your tomorrow is never a promise

Satisfied

What more can I say
What more can I do
You always think there's more
Having so much seems enough
It's still not enough for you
The golden boy
The golden egg
The perfect smile
It's still not enough for you
The great raise
The next in line
The borrowed time
The money galore
And much much more
It's still not enough for you
A house that shines
A career that's divine
A family who cares
A car that flares
It's still not enough for you

But as for me
I know that I am a winner and not a loser
I know that I am a finder and not a keeper
I know that I am a giver and not a taker
I know that I am a doer and not a quitter
So whatever it is that I ever will do
With all that I do
It will never stop ever
Being enough for me

Destiny

I will fly as high as the sky will allow me
I will soar as far as the wind will take me
I will run as long as the roads will lead me
For I understand that the gift of
A mind that travels is an
Endless journey
Limitless boundaries were
Made for those who will search out a matter and
Never stop
Alas, alas
I can see the dawning of a new day breaking forth
Through the last of the night sky and
The rising of a fresh sun
I am standing between what use to be and on the
Verge of what I am to become
From a thought, a prayer, a whisper and a
Glimpse into what is known as
My destiny
It is here that I have seen the birds fly with no wind

I have understood the making of the perfect shape
-Me-
And from the substance by which we forget we
Were formed
Earth to earth and dust to dust
It is through the dying of a man's will that will lead
Him on the path of the straight and narrow
Through much loss comes much gain
And if man will conquer this one
He will forever take his place in this earth and
Fulfill his
Purpose filled life

Momentum

Be punctual, be perpetual
Be persistent and be as prominent men
Never give up, never give in
Never stop living and
Always live from within
Be guided by peace and
Let understanding have
Her perfect way
For as knowledge is truth of a thing
So wisdom is a
Light to those that listen to her
Be not afraid of the unknown
Simply close your eyes and you will see
Have stamina, have strength and
Be as the eagle that rules the sky
Be as the hawk that captures her prey
Above all things
Be vigilant in all that you do
Take nothing for chance
And everything for gain
Be as the dreamer that never stops dreaming
For whatever is that you what to be
BE!

Expressions

Smile while the sun is still rising
Smile while the day is yet young
Smile while your cheeks still hold their perfect
Shape
A smile not only brightens the day of the person who
Gives it
But all those who can see it radiating from eyes, as
The sunshine reflects off the face
A smile covers the hurt and pain and
Prevents them from entering into the heart
As long as you wear a smile
You can never wear a frown
So smile while the day is yet young
Smile while your cheeks still hold their perfect
Shape
A smile says, I'm happy
A smile says, I'm excited
A smile says, I'm in love
A smile looks best on the one who wears it
Most
To say it best, a smile looks pretty on you
So always remember to smile because
God loves you

Determination

So hard sometimes, so high it seems and
So lonely it may feel
Too steep for many
What will it take, must the earth shake
Must the sea rise or will you simply
Open your eyes
These are not ordinary steps
But steps predestined be followed
Foretold by some - only a dream to many
Losing battle after battle
Yet still determined to win
Deep sweat perspired from late nights untold
Finally - the true story - unfolds
What you took for weakness
T'was made my strength
That which you would not
I would and I did
What was an obstacle at first sight
Quickly became my stepping stone
Never a mountain to wide
Never a bridge to long
Never a wall to high
I will never as never is ever

Stop rising to pinnacle of my youth
I will over come
I will succeed
If you slow down
I will pass you by
Nothing, no nothing
Will stop me
For
I am
The CEO of
My success

Believe in Yourself

How is it that everyone
Can see the beauty you create and
Understand your pricelessness but you
How is it that so many of us
When looking around
The sacred corners of our mind
Choose to nestle in the warmth
Our common lives harbor
The same keys that are used
To unlock your future
Can be used to lock your past
If you
As an eagle
Never initiate the leap of faith
Then others will never be awed by the
Gracefulness by which you soar
When as a child
Thought I as a child
But now
Am doing all things through him that
Strengthens me

It is the lifting up of the head
That allows you to
See where rainbows begin and end
But few will find the treasure that await
Those who will diligently search for her
Formed by faith
A spoken word gave you life
And now
You are transformed into every word
You say you will be
You have your life to keep
So live everyday
As if it's your best day alive
With everything to gain and
Your next day will be
A brighter
Tomorrow

Trio Of Hope

Wisdom, knowledge and understanding
Has always been an undeniable trio of hope
That governs this land and the people in it
Without an understanding there is no wisdom and
Knowledge
If one doesn't have knowledge how can he
Apply the understanding which is wisdom
Wisdom is the application of knowledge
Knowledge is the level of understanding of a thing
Understanding is gaining truth of a thing
When all of these hope factors work together
They create what many of us call
Morals
Morals help guide us through each and everyday
Just look around you and you can see the differences
between those who have and follow strong and very
Sound morals
Compared to those who have basic morals and few
Principals, yet even
To those who have none

If your life seems to be challenged at this present
Time
If your life seems destined for failure
Or even if your life appears to be on track
I encourage you to first stop right now this very
Instant…
…He who lacks wisdom let him ask of the Lord
Who giveth to all men…
Ask for the wisdom, then
Begin a regimen of building immediate basic
Principals that you can do very easily
Second, within the first ten minutes
Congratulate yourself on beginning and
Accomplishing something new
Because you have just begun steps to a more
Successful you
When everything else fails and dies
There hope will be
Standing alone
By your side

Progress

Why is it when you try to do something to
Help others
Someone always has something negative to say about
You
Whether you are trying to do something great
Make a change for the better
Enlighten others about a new way or
Simply take a step in a new direction
Somebody isn't going to like what it is you are doing
Somebody isn't going to agree with what it is
That you are trying to accomplish
Somebody isn't going to understand your vision, your
Dream or see clearly your plan
Don't ever let someone else's opinion or viewpoint
Discourage you in any way
The dream or the vision you have isn't for
Anyone else to understand unless they agree
With you totally and work with you closely to
Manifest it into reality
So, don't be discouraged
Don't be dismayed
Don't ever stop trying and don't ever give up

The Heart Matters

Be inspired to write
You never know when you will create your next prize
Write daily if you can or
Even as often as you are moved to if it's more
The more you write
The more you learn to express yourself
Poetry is a form of keeping a private journal
Often opened for everyone to read
It can expose your inner most personal feelings and
Emotions
Your passions, your dreams, your goals,
Your likes, dislikes and even your ambitions
Ultimately, your inner nakedness will be
Revealed for everyone to see
For unseasoned writers, this is nothing to be
Frightened about
Because, most writers want the readers to understand
The point they are making within
The writing

When you can write freely from the heart
Others will also learn about the way you think
Also, learn to enjoy yourself more as you explore your
Candidness
So, always write from the heart and don't be
Discouraged
Just be yourself
Whether you are writing fiction, non fiction,
Romance, drama or poetry
It's not always what you write that readers
Will enjoy
Most times it's more about how you write what
You have to say
That will appeal to readers
The heart matters

Life's Creed

I was born into the world this day that I might
Overcome every object that represents
Challenges in my life, my family and
My business
I was born this day to understand two words
I can
I was born this day to see the vision
I live
I was born this day to know the difference
I make
I was born this day to do the things
I believe
I was born this day into the greatness
I choose
I was born this day to leave behind the things
I pass
I was born this day to conquer the things
I learn
I was born this day to share the legacy
I build

A legacy is something a man leaves behind
That others will remember him by
So always plan ahead and
Look beyond the now
Did you know you can choose to be
Born again today
I was born again this day to live my life
To please
His will

Spiritual

Have you ever wondered if there really is a God in heaven who sits above this world we live thriving, ruling, looking down upon us all?

Well, this chapter is dedicated to all those who would dare open up their finite understanding to the spirit realm where there are no dragons or witches, but very powerful angelic beings and most importantly he who I believe has created everything around us, God almighty. May you be guided to the peace you have been searching for in your life, family and business by the comforting power each poem in this chapter holds. There is a peace which passes all understanding and it only comes from God. I have found that if you just simply trust God, read the Holy Scriptures and allow his Holy Spirit to guide you everyday, then the problems, pressures and issues constricting you won't ever be overwhelming. You will gain a peace deep within your soul by accepting him as Lord and savior of your life. If you have yet to do so, you really don't have anything to lose.

Romans 10:9-11 in the Bible helps us all understand;

9 Because if you acknowledge and confess with your lips that Jesus is Lord and in your heart believe (adhere to, trust in, and rely on the truth) that God raised Him from the dead, you will be saved.

10 For with the heart a person believes (adheres to, trusts in, and relies on Christ) and so is justified (declared righteous, acceptable to God), and with the mouth he confesses (declares openly and speaks out freely his faith) and confirms [his] salvation.

11 The Scripture says, No man who believes in Him [who adheres to, relies on, and trusts in Him] will [ever] be put to shame or be disappointed.

AMP

Romans 10:13

For everyone who calls upon the name of the Lord [invoking Him as Lord] will be saved

AMP

Road to Heaven

Roads lead to places unknown
So many to choose from
So few that leads into destiny's chambers
Run away run away
No place to hide
For all roads do end
What road are you on in this race we call life
What will you be doing when your road
Comes to an end
Winding roads dizzies the mind and creates
Confusion
Only the straight and narrow road will take
You through
Where will you be when your roads comes to
An end
Think about it
God already has
Selah

Shooting Star

Though you left us, you're not so far
Away that you still can't hear
Though you're gone, you're not forgotten
Memories are what you left behind
Memories of the laughter
Memories of the teachings
Memories of the love you shared
Love scattered across a nationwide
A nation covered by
The highest in love
The love of God
Just yesterday I thought about you for
The very first time
I thought about what it must be like - to
Stand behind the clouds - to
Sit behind the blackened sky filled with the ever
Twinkling of the - stars
Just last night I thought about you
Yet again
As I watched you wink at me through a star
A star I never saw before
It was the brightest and the most beautiful star
In the frigid night sky
You set there for awhile
As I wrote this poem

Just then I realized
As I felt the tears racing from my eyes
Only to gather beside my bare brown
Feet in a small pond like shape
That
You will always be where you have always been
In the place where we have always kept you
From the first time you taught us to put you
We will forever remember and never forget
Our secret place, Selah
From this night we vow never to hold you so tight
That you will never be as free as you now are
And as I raised my head
The star was gone
And as I stood to my feet
So was the pain
That's right, I shouted
Shoot on, shoot on
Be free, be as free
As GOD almighty
Has now made you to be

Spirit Of Healing

What you mean to me is more than I can say
What you did for me is more than I can
Imagine
What you brought into my live is more
Than I could ever dream
What you gave to me is more - life
I never imagined how real you really are
But I always dreamed you were
I never held so many thoughts
At one time in my mind
And I never set so many free
I can't explain the way I feel right now
But I must try
I feel so extraordinary, so jubilant
So excited, so free and so - alive
If anyone ever wants to know
What you bring into a life
Above all things it's hope
I never have to dream another dream of you
I never have to think another thought
Whether or not you will be there

I can't seem to stop the waterfall that flows
From my eyes
I can't seem to slow down the thankfulness I feel
For you truly have given me more than
All I possess
I gave you my body and you took it
Swallowed up I was
In a fountain of healing
Stirred up by an angel
And now I will
And now must
Live on

Rising Above It

Looking out over the silent sky
Where the blue and white gather
To create a hazy commingling in the distance
Everything is still here
With not even the flight of a bird to watch
And I
Now standing above the clouds
Gain wisdom
And knowledge pours into my veins
As long as you remain here
Above the clouds
They will forever to the eye remain white
It's only when you go below
That new colors they will show
The storm can never rise above the clouds
No more than problems in life
Rise above the mind
God
Will never allow on us more than we can bear
Even problems in life will not last
As the storm itself
Must always pass
So look high on life

And down on its cares
Until you can clearly see the small billows
In the top of the clouds
They are the answers to the prayers we've
Prayed
Just as pebbles dropped in water make their print in
Art
So God drops answers to prayers
Which must pass through the clouds
Leaving their print for him to know
He's hit the mark

Where Faith Abides

Believe, believe, and just believe
The more you say it
The more you will believe it
The more you believe it
Then the more you can receive from it
Man must believe in this thing he has never seen
With naked the eye
He must look beyond where the eyes do see
To the place that hold no stars and
There is no space
It is here that you will find the true meaning of
Everything that has no understanding
In this place we must all learn to put the things
We can't control and need the most
Whether a cure for cancer,
A prayer for speedily recovery,
An overdue mortgage,
A new job, a change in career,
Favor with a judge or
Simply for Gods ear to be near
These are but a few things
You need find in this place

For Gods golden vials hold many prayers
Though you whisper with not a sound
Though you cry with not a tear
Be not afraid, God still hears
We must learn to love
Trust and obey him
Before and during these times
That your voice will be not as sounding brass
A prayer, without a purpose - will not last
If you are ever in need, come visit here often,
But please make haste and pray the prayer of faith
And then just believe
Because you never know
What tomorrow holds

Peace

So rare are you that my thoughts run deep
So priceless are you
That some give their lives just to have you
I love the beautiful sound you make
Neither tinkle nor drop, no nothing at all
As on the wings of a bird you glide gracefully
Through the air
I need you, I long for you
No sleep will I taste until I have you inside
Oh, how well you pass all understanding
When given by God
A gift you are to any that receive you
Countless lives are preserved that welcomes
Your soft landing
Who can withstand the calm you bring
Mighty are the walls that surround your nature
To know that you are near is to know
That there is hope
Time heals wounds, but you provide the path
Come and allow me to wrap my worries
Around you

And let me but taste of your nurturing ways
For my heart is filled with the anticipation of your
Soon arrival
I read in a word that you can make everything
Around you be still
I relax and take a deep breath when I think of
You (sigh)
You are requested by many and given by God
I find my rest in you
My peace

Where God Lives

Can you imagine?
How high the sun sits in the sky?
Can you imagine?
How deep is the ocean beneath?
Can you imagine?
How vast is the world we live?
For how many corners can man journey and never
Turn?
How high can the naked eye really see?
How free can one's mind - really be?
If you could let go and not fall
If you could hold on yet to nothing at all
And if you really opened your eyes
What would you see?
Can you imagine living where there is no time,
Breathing where there is no air,
And walking where there is no land?
More than what you need is he
Yet not enough of what you want
He is closer than the beat of your heart
Yet further than the mind can imagine

He is a friend to the friendly
And a foe only to the enemy
Closing of the eyes causes you to see and
Opening of the soul allows you to be free
As a tree is nourished beside the brooke,
Reading of this word allows you to be made free
Come learn of me...
All that I am

Praise

It sounds good to the ear
It feels better to the soul
Eyes gleam at the coming of your sound
No rest is given until you arrive
Many wait for your soon arrival
You are soothing to the body and
A delight to the mind
Oh, if man would learn to praise the true God
If man would learn to persevere with praise
Through the times so heavy to the heart
He would soon understand that the key is not
In the anticipation of receiving
The reward of praise
But, can be found in its nature by dwelling in
Her presence
If you want to know how to soar through the
Problems
That simply living life brings, then
Learn to praise God in times when things are
Bad
So that you will learn to live life in times when
Things are good

Living a good life does not promise all
Good times
But, praising God through the bad
Happy and sad
Does in the end
So let your tongue speak praise
Whenever you can

Shadows Of Comfort

Above this world we so carelessly live on
Continues to be witnesses that are compassed
About so great amongst the clouds
They provide the shadows where you often
Hide to find relief
They can quickly give encouragement in times
Of despair,
A smile in times of drought
Allow a ray of hope
To shine upon the times of loneliness to
Enlighten the paths that help show us
-The true way-
The day we live is only but a moment and then
Is soon forgotten
A thought comes and parishes as gently as
The smolder from the wicks end of the candle
That sits upon the stick
Moving on is never easy
But looking back always is
The past is the past as yesterday use to be
Today and is now what it can only forever be
A memory and a thought that wonders
Aimlessly
In the back of the mind trying to escape the
Darkness for which it is bound, but

You must look on the inside and know that
Every continuous step pushes the past
Further behind and leads closer to a brighter
Day
A simple raising of the head causes you to
Breathe fresher air and allows you to see things from
A clearer perspective
A simple pause before you speak helps to
Remember the bridle that governs the tongue
And causes you to speak words that are soft
To the ear
Smile and be glad that you're not dead in the
Yesterdays that use to be
But much more alive in the today that holds
Encouragement, a ray of hope, an enlightened
Path or just a free - second chance
If your day ever seems to be filled with what
Resembles the yesterdays
Just lift your head up and look beyond the skies
And remember, that it is Gods smile that
Causes
The clouds to give us these
Shadows of comfort

Omniscient

One look at my life and I begin to see
The reflections of not only what it use to be
But more of what it has begun to become
You must have known
I would never stop thinking about you
Everyday and every night
You must have known
The first time I confessed you
I would never be able to forget you
You must have known
The first time you touched me
My life would never be the same again
You must have known
That simply because you first loved me
That I could truly love others
But still love you most
You must have known
I would never be able to breathe without
Having you in
My life
For
You are the weight of the thoughts in my mind

You are the caverns which house every beat
Of
My heart
You are the strength of the smile
I hold on my face
And
Because of you
My life will never be the same
Because of you
My life has forever been changed
Because of you
My life is a reflection of your enduring love
Everlasting mercy and
Encompassing grace
So
I ask you again
To tell me
That you knew
All along

Love

&

Emotional

There's really nothing more exciting than poetry that expresses true and even sometimes deep sentimental feelings. Anyone who has read the novel "Romeo and Juliet" by author William Shakespeare would know the importance of this style of poetry. He captivated the readers by a revealing love affair that many still shed a tear just thinking about. Romantic poetry releases power that reaches deep within the soul and pierces the heart.

There is no greater love than this…While we were yet sinners Christ died for us. If you really want to find some of the earliest styles of this poetry, then grab a Holy Bible and take a short journey to the book of "Psalms" and read it completely through. This book in the Bible reveals a love affair between a mere mortal man (King David) and a loving God he has never seen. To this day it remains one of the single most talked about love affairs ever.

I'm sure you'll agree that if you really love someone then there is not a more passionate way to express your true feelings than using creative writing techniques. Choose words from your own heart that best describe what it is you are trying to say.

You will soon find that no card can truly say it the way you can and so will your love.

Practice writing this style as often as you can and you will soon understand that it will open the door to a whole new world of writing. Write about the love you have in your life, whether it's a person, a flower, a house, a beautiful city, a favorite place, a store, a house, a vehicle or even nature. You'll find it easier to write about the things you love because you really don't have to search for so many words. Being moved to write this chapter, I opened my heart for you to see and I hope that you will to for others.

Wedding Vow

Standing here looking into your stare and
Into the eyes that glare
I feel the nervousness in the grip your hands
Do hold around my fingers
If I could whisper a prayer to you
I would
If I could whisper a song to you
I would
If i could light up the world to watch you smile
Forever
I would
If I could give you the world on a stick
I would
Everything in this world will soon belong to
Us
With my life
I promise to live for you
With my body
I promise to thirst for you
With all my love
I promise to long for you

Whether knots by sea
Whether time by sky
Whether miles by road
Nothing
Shall create a distance so great between us
That I would not travel
I brought to you today a vow
That I might keep the memory of this day
Forever in my heart
In vowing to have and to hold
It is the woman who has that which was given
It is the man who holds that which to give
It is both who share in the receiving of each gift
I give you me and you give me you
The light holds no boundaries to which our love can
Reach
Time cast no spell on the age our love can
Grow
I now look into the eyes which reflect the images that
Radiate straight from the heart
With all the strength I have
With all the air I breathe
With all the courage I hold
I say to you on this day
Our day

Fairy tales is what we first believed in when
We were children
But only the mature in heart can dream a dream
As beautiful as the one I now behold
I believe in God
I believe in miracles
I also believe in
Our love
I
Do
Now and forever more
I always will

Making Of Love

What is love but unlimited intimate
Moments in time
Moments created, shared and
Enhanced over time
For only time will tell my love
How much I need thee
Yes Yes Yes
My desire is to taste of thy sweet love tonight
But first
We must sit by the candle light
My desire is to feel the warmth of your body
Rubbing against mine
But first
We must dine, enhanced by the finest of wine
My desire is to connect two intermittent
Lives together
But first
We must remember our commitment to
Love, honor and trust
My desire is to be closer to you
Than your mother was just before the beginning of
Your time

But first
We must die from within and give from without
My desire is to love thee with the love
That I have for no other
But first
We must breathe the same air and our hearts
Must beat the beat of a single stick drummer
My desire is to light up the world with
Your smile
But first
We must form one glorious light that can
Make even the faintest star twinkle
It will be the glow that others remember us by
That is how you will know
Our love shines

Perfect Gift

Love is a priceless donation
Sown into the lives of
Everyone around us
If we cease to love
Love will cease to be
And the giving of a gift will just
Be a small token with a price tag
If everyone purposes in his own heart to give
That which is good, perfect and acceptable
The act of giving would elevate to the will of God
Life is a love gift when it is shared as
The donation of a vital organ or
Even ones own blood
Your body becomes love when it is donated to
Another in the state of holy matrimony
As two lives become one
So let love, see love, be love
And you to will be loved as it will
Come back to you
So in all your giving
Give everything you can

From your hat
Your coat
Your slipper to your hand
Hold nothing back
Hold nothing in
Every lover must love to give
That which he can
And if you promise to give
The greatest in love
Time, life, body and soul
In return my gift to you will be
Eternal love
From heaven above

First Love

I can't deny the feelings I have in my heart for
You
I can't seem to shake the thoughts that run
Perilously through my mind
My thoughts of you have been known to run
Deep
The love that I carry for you journeys endlessly as if no
End to all time
I am left with the memory of your smile
The simple way you combed your hair
The scent of your body on my pillow and
In the air
The sound of your laughter which echo's from
The walls
I will always cherish the moments in time we
Shared that I still hide in my heart
I gaze into the deep thoughts I have of you
As if a beautiful picture that sits on the wall
The years pass and the thoughts become fewer
And is now only a shadow to a new love which is fuller
The love we once knew has faded to a feeling
That's doomed
Until finally, there's no more room

French Farewell

It's so hard 2 say I love
It's so hard 2 say I miss you
It's even harder 2 say good-bye
This one thing I never wanted 2 say
This one day I never thought I'd see
So emotional at times and so sentimental
Oh the memories that cross my mind
I find it hard for me 2 believe that
The love we shared can never be repaired
Time and time again we tried
Only 2 hide behind the lies
If I could wash away the memories
If I could wipe away all the shed tears
Would it make a brighter day
Would the sun rise and never set or
Would we have ever tasted the night again
Tellement voici à notre amour
Tellement voici à notre amour
Tellement voici à notre amour
Au revoir'
Pour toujours je t'aime

First Kiss

When I first saw you it was your smile
That drew me
When I saw you closer it was your eyes that
Kept me
When I got to know you it was
The thoughts of holding you
That warmed my heart
Let me hold you my love
For I long to wrap my arms around you
As I hold you ever so close, leaving no space
I feel myself rising as I imagine the possibilities that
The silent night still holds
Can we press closer tonight
Thoughts of a kiss
Yes yes yes
I will wait for the perfect time on the right day
The gentle breeze on a peaceful walk
The perfect moment in time
Then, as I close my eyes
I inhale deeply and pause
I gently press against thy lips with mine
And the tingling of my skin causes
My tiny hairs to rise

I then exhale
While the arms I have wrapped
Tightly around you are
Used to pull you ever so closer
I slowly open my eyes and
I see you the first time
For the first kiss
May it last and never end
Until next time
We make this kiss
Again

Our Song

When I hear that special rhythm I can't explain
The way it makes me feel
No other sound commands my body to
Respond like this
I have come to understand that it's not in the
Rhythm, nor in the rhyme
But in every corner of my mind
Here is set aside a place that is closed to all
With an exception to the playing of this song
I can not escape the thoughts that prevail
As this moment in time continue to unwind
No matter the space, no matter the place
It sets the mood, it creates the moment
I can not deny the feelings I hide
As it plays on
As if a soldier standing watch over his fellow
Brothers
So does the tear that slowly crawls across my
Face guard against the emptiness I feel
No matter how far markers on highways may
Separate us the effect is still the same
This one moment in time
I will think about you more than

Anything else in the world
I will give you more of me than I have for
Myself
As long as I hear this song, our song
I will be lost in the memories of my mind
I will pull you closer in my thoughts
I will hold you tighter in my heart
I will make virtual love to you in my mind
And as this song nears the end
I can't help but remember why and
What caused us to be where we now are
-Apart-
The one thing we did do right more than all
The others is that we created a song
A song that will last till the last moment and
The last beat of either heart
Then and only then will this song die from
Within
And never tug at this lonely heart ever again
So excuse me
If I seem lost from time to time
I've not lost my mind
I'm just listening to the rest of
Our song

The Unexpected

I didn't expect to feel this way
I now feel about you
I didn't expect our friendship to flow
Let alone grow
I didn't expect for my eyes to look at another
The way I now look at you
I never thought that there could be a love so
Strong that even a wounded heart would
Mend
When I look into your eyes I often lose my
Thoughts to a dreamy stare
When I think of you I see your images
Running wildly through my mind
How does love make a woman feel so
Loveable?
A man act so invincible and a couple be so
Inseparable?
If you want to know
Come, take a journey into my heart and follow
The river that leads to my soul
There you will understand how the feelings I
Have for you grow and see
Where all rivers end

Must flow
I will no longer hide behind this waterfall of love
That brings an end to the nights rule by
The setting of the stars and the rising of the sun
I now know and understand that it's all
Because I didn't want to expect anything other than
Who
You are and what you mean to me
Not just in my heart but also in my mind
And when I didn't expect to find a thing
I found the greatest gift of all
I found you
For it is written that …as we think, so are we…
GOD made me free and
You set my mind free

The Love Inside You

I was asked this question and I looked to myself
The question I was asked to which I needed to
Reply
What do you love?
So simple to the sound and yet very profound
As my head I hang down toward the ground
Silent at first, then a loud outburst
As I lift my head with a look that was stead
I said
I love the apples from the tree which sparkles in
The eye
I love the flight of the bumble bee which buzzes
Right by
I love the colors in the sky as the sun sets in the by
And by
I love to watch the way a merry heart creates a silent
Smile
I love to listen to the laughter that of a jolly ole soul
I love to watch the way your hair reacts against
The blowing of the wind

I love to hear the song from the birds and how
They dance in the sky
I love the closeness that I feel when nestled in
Your arms
I love the way your eyes move when centered on
My charm
I love the freshness of the air after the rain
Ceases to fall
I love the smell of the rose in its perfect shape
I love the touch of your lips on my ear and the sound
Of your breath so near
I love to imagine the possibilities of the
Determined mind, the enduring heart and the
Courageous soul
But most of all
I love everything there is to know
All about the love we show
So if ever you are asked
This question you may hear
Think more about the things
That will make more love appear

ReUnited

In first meeting
A kiss is shared
We reminisce on this
The parting of the heart
Causes great sorrow
A lasting effect no man or woman can fill
As if the earth tilted
We live again what was lost back then
Joining of hearts
Mending to every part
Here we are
Now together
Forever

Journey Within

Come go with me into my paradise
Where the winds are calm and the breeze is
Soothing
Come enjoy the comforts of my escape
Where no man knows the fullness there of
Where the lands are priceless
Where the air is crystal
Come relax in my plentiful waters of fulfillment
Let the rivers run through your hair
Feel the warmth of my embrace and
Slowly let yourself go as I
Command your senses to be enhanced
By the gentle blowing
Of my whispers around your mind
Close your eyes
For this is a journey into the depths of the soul
Where there is the purest of pure
The calm of calms
The still of stills and
The peace of all peace

No understanding is needed there
Just trust that in following your heart
You are where you want to be
In my arms
In my presence
With me

Essence Of Love

The color of love is often overlooked by a heart
That sees no light
If a heart can see no light
Then it will never be able to understand
The true nature of love
Love cannot be felt by a heart that feels no pain
No more than a heart full of hate
Understand the real beauty of color
Though eyes may close
Color can still be seen
If you ran away to hide in a secret place
Feelings still follow you the same
Colors can not be erased from the mind
They follow you to your pillow
And bring life to your dreams
One never thought to look at love this way
But then again, love never said to look
No one can outrun the colors of race

For it abides deep beneath the skin and flows
Silently through the veins
It is there
Where priceless color thrives
Creating a rhythmic beat inside the heart
With pure love
There is no hate
Favorite to many
Surely to me
You are the color of love
That means most to me

Fantasy

I'm thinking of you
Thinking of how you do what it is you do
The roads, the skies and the sea
So long, so high and so deep
All relate to the ways
I think about you
As the mathematical minds wonder
And the psychological minds run deep
So I think about you
It's been said that maybe, just maybe
I think too much about you
I can't help myself
So I will allow
To fly free as a bird
Straight as an arrow
My many, many thoughts
The oh so too many thoughts
I have of you
I wish to be led closer to spending more than just
My thoughts
Forever with you

While You Were Out

How many thoughts of you must I think till I see
You again?
How many sleepless nights must I attain?
Too many sheep to count and so many pictures
Of you running through my mind
Waiting to share with you again
The true feelings of my heart
Missing you every moment we're apart
Love calls our names to be one
I often wonder
I often dream of the days ahead
Days filled with not just thoughts
Days filled with not just dreams
But, days filled and overflowing with the sweet
Honey melon juices of our love intertwined as
One mighty river
The river runs through our veins and
Into our hearts
On this river of love are you and I
Living together, forever in
Our world

5Os Lovers

Though many years have pasted
Two lives have managed to become one
And a love has remained strong
The love has weathered the trials
The love has over come many obstacles
The love has endured tough times
Now we stand here together
Representing a love that will last forever
If I roll my chair to the highest
Mountains peak
If I travel solo across life's
Lonely highways
Even if I sail my boat across
The sea all alone
I'd will that you were there
This life has not always been easy
But it has always been good
Because we've been together
Through fifty one years
Our love is still secure
Through fifty more
I could endure
I know one day

A knock will come to our door
And this love we know here
Will be no more
We will travel through the clouds
And land in open hands
My eyes will open wide
And I will see you there
Again
So be patient my sweet darling
Be patient my kind love
This time I promise
We will never part
Again

Closure

What did I do
To cause you to love me this less
I have tried to understand
But can't quite figure out
What has caused this love to come to an end
My life I did change
My ways I did bend
All to make myself in your eyes look comely again
With a ring I did wed a perfect mate I chose
To live together forever in a land of love
Our fairytale
Who would have imagined it would come to
This
One love separated from the other
By an invisible impenetrable wall
That neither one could explain
So I write to say as I shed one last tear
I thought about you
As I remembered your smile
I will miss the sound of laughter you gave
Your presence is missed and the kids good night kiss

I wish there was a way for surely I would rewind and
Capture all the tears I watched fall
Through the years
When you think of me always know
I did truly love you
For now, this love I set free
That in your heart you may see
That if you really love someone
Finally set them free
I set you free to smile again
To laugh again
To live again
To be again
To see again
To dance again
To run again
And finally
To love again
When you think of me a second time
Shed not a tear
For if I don't set you free
I will never be
I have miles to travel that will lead someday
To a path ahead, where we may once again meet in
Some way

If I haven't told you in awhile
I did really love you then
May God who gives grace
No matter the race
Give to you also
Grace
May you have peace in your endeavors
And a lamp unto your feet
Keep GOD before you
And never let go
Goodbye forever
My love
Lost

Partner for Life

Can you understand the steps
That I must take
Look ever so closer as to where I walk
My feet
They walk the walk that rings in my ears
My ears
Drum the sound I send from my heart
My heart
Beats the beat I imagine in my mind
My mind
Thinks the thoughts I stream through my eyes
My eyes
See the steps that are not really there
So I close my eyes and release my soul
Smoothly, swiftly and gently I flow
For this time my feet will never meet
The grounds warm heat
I set my body in motion
As I dream a dream
So I go

I will not be satisfied
Until every curve of your body
Has met every thought in my mind
Until my heart has been warmed by the quiet
Breeze blowing around your presence
I love you so
Will you ever know
I hold on to every moment of time
I will follow where you lead
I will run to where you are
In the end
I will always stand right next to you
In support for all you choose to do

Humorous

Jazzy

Personal

&

Other

Have you ever had a really good dream that you wished would never end?

Have you ever wondered what it would be like if all of a sudden you had everything you ever wanted?

It's the same feelings an author can experience when he/she begins to write and the pens flow seems to never end creating what I call "The Poet Zone©." Exciting as it may sound, it is truly much more exhilarating to experience this moment personally. This natural experience generally surfaces when the writer has begun to mature in their writing and has also begun to understand their style of writing as well.

A poet's style of writing matures on its own, but I have found that it matures quicker for poets when they (amateur or seasoned) read their writings aloud. For this exercise I highly recommend participating in "Open-Mic" poetry readings. You might not feel comfortable with this exercise at first and is not a prerequisite to experiencing the Poet Zone. It is merely is a way to allow the experience to mature more rapidly. Reading aloud in front of others will allow your ears to be trained to hear what others hear, as if listening to a spoken word from a third parties viewpoint. This will also help build a must have ability to all starving writers.

Confidence, once this writing ability is truly accepted and most recognizable within yourself first and then to others, you will then begin to bloom.

I'm sure you have heard the saying if you love something set it free; this is also true as it relates to poetry. Set your poetry free by writing as often as you can for beginners. Others might write as often as they feel moved to write, even if you have to write on a napkin or on a piece of tissue paper. Move quickly to capture the moment. Soon you will learn to parallel your writing style with the way your mind really thinks and you will definitely notice an improvement in your writing. As you continue to practice these exercises you can also incorporate more of your hurts, joys, hardships, dreams, ambitions, relationships, friendships, experiences and anything else you so choose to include. The goal is to permanently defeat the Goliath called writers block. I believe writers block is just a myth and a term that some writers use when they are completely burned out, frustrated about a project, don't have enough fresh ideas or are just plain ol' too tired.

The mind works twice as hard as the physical body does and many believe the rate to be slightly higher than that.

Usually young writers don't understand how to use creative writing techniques to continue writing through tough times. Using creative writing techniques can bring balance to your writing as also taking a much needed rest can help clear your mind. Some idea things you can do to help enhance your writing styles would be to take a nice long walk in a favorite park or on favorite beach, read a new book, take a much needed vacation or trip to a relaxing location and don't forget to laugh and laugh some more. Laughter is like a medicine and can help heal the mind, body and soul.

It is not suggested that you force yourself to write all day everyday, unless you have trained your body and your mind to write for hours and hours at a time. This technique requires much practice, patience and endurance to achieve and isn't for everyone.

I took my time when writing these sets of poems.

This chapter has the most styles of poems because I used many different creative writing techniques to create these poems.

So sit back and enjoy them and most importantly, have fun and set your mind free

Journey to Freedom

It all started back then
When we were forced to comprehend
What the white force was that had suddenly
Befallen us
Overtaken in the night
In a dry and thirsty land
Against such evil
We could not defend

Taken from a land
That was known to our eyes
Never saw such beauty then
Never saw such beauty since

As a people we grew wiser
And began to learn the ways
Overcoming every obstacle
Soon,
We began to count the days

Sold into slavery
Brought into abuse
A noose so tight
We could not loose

Lived in nature
Washed like swine
Slept in grasses
And ate less than divine

Encouraged by God
With songs sang from the heart
Soon reading and writing
We knew
We were smart

BeatN, kickD and women often raped
CursD, bruisD and feet swollen from gout
We knew then
There was only one way out

So we looked to the heavens
And began to say
I will lift my head up
I will stand my ground

And then release these solemn words
I ain't goN back down!

You see
We'd had enough of the cotton pickN
Hound dog huntN
Broad daylight hangN
Just tryN to escape
The pleaZ the mastA attitude
So we could finally B
What God intended for all of us to B
Free!

For two hundred years
Black men were
Hung, slung and killed with the gun
Y should a father have to loose is only son just
Because ignorant black fools keep picking up
The same tool today and continue the slaughter

That's Y we must all unite
And B of one color
So that the young lives that live behind us
In this way
We will lose not a one

And so that all Gods people
Will began to lift up their heads
One and all
And finally stand together
And release this solemn sound

WE HAVE OVERCOME

WE HAVE OVERCOME

WE HAVE OVERCOME TO-DAY

(REPEAT THREE TIMES)

Live in the past no more

Visions Of Beauty

I first saw you from a distance
And as a rising tide
I just couldn't seem to take my eyes off you
I glanced at your figure
And I somehow seemed to smell the fragrance
That surrounded your presence
The bronze likeness of your skin tone
Reminded me of the sunsets
Warm glow back on the islands I know
The thoughts of your fruits enhanced
The passing visions in my mind
My sight became clearer
You seemed to be drawn nearer
Selah
As a delicate flower blooms
Early in the misty dewed day
With just a touch of sun
You smiled
Just like a Picasso painted picture
A Van Gogh created masterpiece
You are a lasting beauty
For lifetimes to come

Change Of Heart

Why didn't I say what I really wanted to say
When I saw you
I had a chance to
But the moment just didn't feel right
To many people around
The room filled with all the wrong people
I wish I could say
What I really want to say
But I just
Walk away
I try not to look into your eyes
When I stare into your face
What I feel when I'm around you makes my body
Tingle
And my -
Heart race
These moments in time were not meant to be
I wish to say
What I have to say
So that my words I may
Set free

As I think alone I gain more boldness
Trying to find what I left behind
I search for you
Only to find you not
Now that I can say
Now that I will say what I would not say
Now that I have the boldness of a tiger
Now that I have the courage of a lion
Now that I have the strength of a thousand men
My words are but in vain
If I should never utter again
I whisper into the wind
The three words my lonely heart longs to be relieved
Of

Nah, never mind

Small Viewer

From a Childs eyes you can see so much
You can see dirty hand prints left on the wall
From a Childs eyes you can see so much
You can see that the toilet seat
Has a big black hole in the middle
From a Childs eyes you can see so much
You can see dads pants continue to fall
And mom's dresses don't quite fit at all
From a Childs eyes you can see so much
You can see grandma and grandpa's teeth
Swim in a jar
From a Childs eyes you can see so much
You can see dad spanking mom in bed
Boy, she must have been bad
From a Childs eyes you can see so much
You can see the cool magnifying glasses on grandpa's
Eyes
From a Childs eyes you can see so much
You can see that mom and dad
Really do care
Even if they swear

From a childs eyes you can see so much
You can see when auntie bends down to kiss
You - boy those huge things sure are soft
From a childs eyes you can see so much
You can see that every year mom and dad
Keeps shrinking - this is cool
From a childs eyes you can see so much
You can see that dad keeps telling your
Uncle Sam to luck off
I think it's because he keeps pointing at him
From a childs eyes you can see so much
So much so
The memories
Last
For a lifetime

Love Worth Healing

I open my eyes only to see the very things
That I don't want to see
I open my ears only to hear the very things
That I don't want to hear
I open my mouth only to speak the very things
That I don't want to speak
I open my mind only to think the very things
That I don't want to think
I open my heart only to love the very things
That keeps hurting me
Why is it that every time I open up
I allow myself to be hurt again
I can't seem to stop the stream of love that
I have for you
From penetrating the brokenness in my
Wounded heart
Why can't the hurt that I allowed myself to be
Hurt by you and the brokenness in my
Wounded heart which penetrated the stream
Of love
I had for you
Enough

Why is it that every time I open
My eyes
My ears
My mouth
My mind and
My heart
That I
Keep asking myself
Why
Why can't this cycle of
Mad love triangle
Stop looping around
The corners of my
Thoughts
I will these thoughts
This time
To end
So let's get counseling
Let's pray for a miracle
So that our love
This time
Would finally
Mend

Life Within

From a seed you grew and
To think at first, nobody knew
Silent and still
Peaceful at will
There was life in the seed
Carefully nurtured
Fed the right foods
Still nobody saw
The miracle in brew
Nobody knew
But me and you
So silent and still
So peaceful at will
There was life in the seed
From a small sign of a bulge
To a full frontal blimp
How soon they all knew
There was live in the seed

So active at will
You can't be still
Oh my
Will you come today
Soon brought forth
You were heading due north
From the doctors hands
To my loving arms
Swaddled so cute
Who would think
From a seed you grew
There you now lay
Silent and still
Peaceful at will
Now everyone can see
The life that was in the seed

Benefits Of Nourishing

If you nourish your crop
It will soon yield a great harvest
If you nourish a plant
It will bloom and then blossom
If you nourish a puppy
It will grow to love you
If you nourish your team
They will win you the game
If you nourish your employee
They will honor you with time
If you nourish your scalp
Your hair will grow fuller and fuller
If you nourish your body
You will help sustain your days
If you nourish your mind
You will gain wisdom untold
If you nourish an idea
It will manifest in riches to come

If you nourish your spouse
You will sleep well at night
If you nourish your house
It will out live you in days
If you nourish your spirit
You will live in heaven foretold
If you nourish your children
They will grow up to be just like you
And they too
Will help nourish
The world around you
So before the sun sets
Before the moon rise
Do something to nourish a thing
You behold
With your eyes

Amazing Grace

You go by so effortlessly
You seem at times never to end
And all to quick at others
Whether good times or bad times
You never change
You are to kings
The glory of their kingdom reign
You are to a child
Hardly a thought
You are to this world we live
The most priceless token there is
Who can understand the wonder you are
Who can resist the precious moments you
Allow
You stand the test
You forgive all sins
You heal all wounds
You calm many storms
You mend broken hearts
You last through the years
You overcame each obstacle
You endured through the pain

And finally
Through it all
You've always
Made me smile again
Everyone at some point
Has been thankful for your existence
No one has seen your face
No one can explain your vastness
There is no story that man should lie
There is no tale that others should cry
Only moments in life
That I am thankful for
In one way or another
We're all glad you're around

Speak Softly

A word fitly spoken is like apples of gold
In pictures of silver
And a word spoken in due season
How sweet it is
Words have long been said
Some of which help lift the head
Be careful
Words jump, people they bump
All end up according to every word
We shed

Sculpture

Looking down on mother earth
From high above in the sky
I can see mans determination
To fulfill Gods first commands
Go, be fruitful and multiply
And replenish the earth
By doing a fly by
I get a view from a bird's eye
And with every separating of the trees that pass
I catch a glimpse of this settling word in action
Gods' infinite wisdom coupled with his
Awesome and creative thinking
He carefully sculpted the lands
Using only his bare hands
He justly divided the deep
He gave cold, wet, hot and dry
The power to rule in distant regions
Gone by
I give glory to our creator
I give to honor him that is due
In his word is read

That while on the seventh day he rested
He still reined king uncontested
Man with his lack of understanding
Could not undertake so great a task
So great a plan
Now sitting back on his throne
He gets glory
As man gains wisdom
Into the moral
Of this story

Gratitude

For all the good you are to me
For all the ways you have helped me
My heart is and forever will remain
Grateful
I keep counting all the years as months
All the months as days
All the days
I count as many moments
Because
You've been there when the rain of tears
Fell from my face
You've noted me in my frailest state
You've watched me climb out of brokenness and
Walk into success
When I overcame sickness and graduated
Magna cum laude in gratefulness
You were there
Thanks to you I am who I now am
And because of you
I have been where I've gone

Now I must watch the skies
For they hold the paths to my greatest quest
Though some live long
Others die young
Whether in the middle or at the end
I will never loose the thoughts I hold of you
There is no easy way to say it
As I hold back the tears
As my throat chokes each swallow
With few words to say it best
Thank You
Thank you
Thank you
For all that you have come to be to me
Time reveals that our journey must come to an
End
From earth to space
From space to glory
That is where we will spend
The rest of our story
God bless you

Missing My Pillow

Where have all the feathers gone
I left you this morning
Now I have you not
Have you one feather
Have you none
Are you hiding in the sweet abyss
Where there is no time and
There is no space
Alone in the dark
So silent
So still
I often wonder where you are
And when I can come back to you
I find myself
Looking, searching and patiently
Waiting for the sounds of joy you create
For I long to hear the laughter you bring
Selah,
I remember the times you hid my tears
So many times you muffed the pain

So still you lay
Never to run
To a bed a mate
To a head much comfort
I say my prayers and lay down my head
It is there I find you in your perfect shape
Soon a sigh
Then a yawn
The night is then chased away by the rising sun
So soft and warm
You are security and shelter
To me you are and will always be
My feathers

The Prize

Happy is the man the findeth a good thing
Oh, woman you are an unmistakable phenomenon
Often called in ancient philosophy
The most remarkable being ever created
Ever wonder why
Why God kept this design from man until he awoke
Form a long slumbered sleep
Why did the God who is infinite, omnipotent,
Omniscient and omnipresent
Decide to go back as one might say
To create another being after he had already
Created everything
Including man
Even man can't figure her out and doesn't know
Why
Oh woman
True you are
Expressive you be
In my heart and
In my eyes
Impressive to me

I can see why God saved the best creation for last
Oh man, before you decide to undertake the
Journey into the heart of this one
Think twice and then again
Because God only dealt with the woman after he
Had already rested awhile
So rare
So priceless is the woman who cares, shares
And who offers life to those without
She is the shadow of a mans heart and the keeper of
Us all
She helps us understand those things so deep
Inside us
Man had named all the other creatures across
The land
But was not honored to name this one
I did try
I now understand
The rib that was taken from man
Can once again be joined again
To look at you is to behold
The perfect gift from God to man

Charity

You might think that trust is just a feeling that
Someone has
You may think that love is just another
Senseless emotion
Though we strive to survive in this land
So many of us call home
We are alive
Think of the people that you sometimes pass
By
Sometimes they beg and others they cry
God created every creature, then man
He gave him dominion to rule this land
So that people like us
When asked won't lie
They'd rather that you would
Just walk by
Living in alleys and on the not so pretty
Streets like Broadway
They are the filthy dirty smelly people
Whose buckets are filled with more nickels
And dimes from people who care
More than others

Being created equal as the Good Book and
Constitution reads
Everyone has been touched by the
Same hands that breathed life into us all
We have liberty
We have justice
They just need a family
The next time you're walking down an alley or
Broadway
Remember that
Trust is not just a feeling that someone has
Love is not just another senseless emotion
Now you see
That sometimes it takes
People like them
To help people like us
Really understand that we were all born free
So, whenever you can share with your
Fellow brothers
Who may have less than you
If only kind words or the shake of a hand
Give to your local Red Cross or charity today thank
You and
May GOD bless you

Voice

Come, set your voice free and allow it to abide
In the canal of my hearing
Come, let your song vibrate off the drummers drum
That harmonize with the guitars' strum
I can see the rainbow that your smile creates showing
All the love and joy you bring
Oh, how radiant of a glow that covers your face
As your words continue to radiate off the hearts,
The ears, the minds, the thoughts of those that are
Captivated by the illuminating rays that surround
The stage
I can feel the rhythms' heat as it warms every bone
And I make my moves like a
Double-jointed king
Who can keep up with the flow I create
It doesn't matter how high, low or in between
Soul, country, jazzy or just plain ol' R&B
Whatever the range
I know you've got it covered
You can go with the best of the best and not
Even thinking about all the rest
Because your voice is as strong as an angel

As soft as feather
As heavy as bass on a drummers drum
And as light as a
Cirrus cloud
Your voice challenges the imagination to try
And find more than an imaginary line that
Separates the place where the stars rest and moon
Hangs
Between the place we call space and the wonder we
Dream of called heaven
So again I say to you
Come, set your voice free
And allow it to nullify the distance that
Remains between those who have not heard
And can not hear from others who bask and
Indulge themselves in the richness of your sounds
This is where you need to be
Close to others but right next to me
So sing
Sing baby
Sing

The Silence Of Creation

Thru windows we can see the opening to a
New dimension
Windows allow all light to shine thru
Thru windows we can see the clear sky blue
On the other side is freedom we presume
Never quite knowing the sorrow that looms
Gazing up in the yonder sky
Counting every cloud gently sailing by
A place where dreamers dream
The wind collides
The night spies
The trees clap
The birds fly and
All of nature sings
As if watching a silent movie in a wide open field
It's all but lost in the silence it yields
And so all of nature screams still go unheard

What's on the other side of your windows?

Poetry

We are because we live and strive to be
What no other man can be
If we cease to strive then we cease to become
That certain thing that we were predestined to
Be
When we reach those dreams we have dreamt
Those things we have idolized and
Those set goals finally attained
Then
More lives will blossom and benefit
From a life that has fulfilled its purpose
So let us help one another by
Sharing thoughts
Sharing dreams
Sharing ideas
Sharing everything we can imagine
About our lives
About this world
About this universe
Then
It only makes sense
To be called as it forever already is
Poetry

Rocks

Rocks is the word that comes to mind
When I think of you
My world is what rocks with you in it
I can see how nature rocks by looking at all the
Beauty it creates
I can even see how your world rocks by looking
At the glow that sparkles around your finger
It's still good to know that there is
Someone to thank
For all the good that surrounds the day
Whether so tiny as a thought or
So silent as a prayer
No matter what
You always seem to come through
When I need you most
Happy are my thoughts of you
Smiles are what you bring
Joy is what you help create
For all that you are and all I want you to be
In your very own way
Everything you do always
Rocks

Pride

Though you're walking tall
You're actually very small
Have you taken a look lately
Oh, how is sweet the smell of success
For it lingers on long after
The moment is gone
It can cause you to look far ahead
Yet not in front
It can cause you to walk swiftly
With your head toward the sky
Never understanding people as you
Unknowingly just pass them by
Glancing without truly looking
No time to pause
The smell of a rose you will not know
Time is all you want to have
To follow the smell that has led you thus far
But being blinded by success
We must remind you
About the importance of how to treat those left
Behind you

Be mindful
Be compassionate
Be all that you never thought to be
Believe in the heart
It will lead to righteousness
The mind will not plot deceitful days
When you submit to God
Who guides your ways
Always remember the steps you take
So you will never have to see them again
Give only from where you can not see
Where there is an abundance of warmth that
Fills the soul
The heart
Where peace and love flows freely
Then the smile you smile
Will come from within and
Not just fill the face from without
Learn these things
And do not pout
They will help keep you from falling
On your face
And from losing the bout

Seasons

I rake the leaves from between the rocks
I rake the leaves from between the trees
I rake the leaves from behind the bushes
I stop for a moment to notice the silence all
Around me
It's easy to see the beauty of this season
The squirrels so busy
The ravens standing guard over the now barren trees
Can you hear their cry?
For it fills the air as the crisp leaves clap
Together blowing where the wind may
Missing are the tiniest of things
Like the mighty ants now gone from the scene
A puppy barks and dash from side to side
As he chases the wind that carries the leaves
With summer gone and fall in full bloom
Ole' winter waits behind
To show us more beauty not gloom
Each season has its beauty hidden inside
If you look closely you will see it
All on the outside

Take time to notice
The beauty that God allows the seasons to bring
You will find comfort in knowing
That his goodness and grace
Is all around us
And in a moments notice
In the blink of an eye
So the seasons change in our lives
Learn to share your world and believe that
You
Can help make heaven on earth possible
In someone's life
Because you can

Our Nation Lives

When a leader dies
His legacy and honor will rise
Though in body he leaves us
Through his character
His words in action yet cleave to us
He overcame failure, follies and faint
As he stood
He found courage and stamina through
Forbearance and faith
And for many years mightily he stood
He looked out over the land to see
What things that you and I should be
Now counting the blessings
We can all understand
That if it were not for him
We'd all just be bland
He has seasoned us with the seasoning of his will
As we rise in belief
As we encounter distant lands
As we walk into the knowledge
That he used to enlighten this land
And as we become what

Maya Angelou, Emily Dickinson, Edgar Allen Poe
All who used their creative artistic abilities to
Describe
A land where we all live and have
Freedom of expression
Freedom of religion
Freedom to become everything
The mind is willing to become
A land where brave men and women live and die
A land that will forever be known for the beauty it
Creates
What every president that have gone on
Before us said
From
Washington, Jefferson to Ulysses S Grant
Roosevelt, Truman, Eisenhower and Ford
Something for us to see
A legacy left to becloud us
A nation we are to be proud of
A land worthy to be called
America the great

Airport Blues

Sitting in the airport
Watching all the planes go by
With nothing more to do
Than to try and keep myself occupied
I pick up a USA today
With all the news about yesterday
I even catch a glimpse of CNN
It helps put today more in view
What am I to do?
You see
I arrived here three hours ago
Hoping to escape the traffic jams
The extra long lines
The waiting times for a cup of brew
Or even a sip of tea from SBC
It's now early in the day
Everyone seems to have found their way home thru
The night, but me
I'm all checked in
I've got my boarding pass in hand
I'm ready to go
At least I thought so

Here I now still sit after at first
In a hurry to go
I barley made my bus with a minute to show
I've utilized my cell phone till my ear sweat in discus
And then began to ache
Even that couldn't crucify the time between
My early arrival and expected departure
Leaning back in the barely cushioned chair
As if sitting in a doctors office who always
Runs at least an hour behind
I began to clearly see
I've got the airport blues
They told me to come early to avoid long lines
I did that
They told me three oz, one item and one clear bag
I did that
They told me to always have your boarding pass at
Hand and your ID ready to show
I did that too
They never told me what to do to avoid
The airport blues
I try to close my eyes and reminisce on this
As if only a moment had passed
That famous southwest bell goes "dung"

The announcer calls the final boarding
For my flight out trip
I quickly jump to my feet with my bag in hand
Once again I found myself in a hurry to go
Whew, I made my plane with a minute to show
Sitting back in my seat I began to laugh
HA, Ha, Ha
I did it again
I close my eyes
And failed to see the clues
I just beat
The airport blues

Da' Steppers

Where have all the steppers gone
I give a root root to all the rhythmic people
Still out there tryn to git ther grove on
Seems like just yesterday I was numbered
Amongst the crowd
Watching the gracefulness by which you flow
Its, its kinda jazzy
Kinda, kinda classy
The way you make ur body one with the music's heat
The rhythmic beat
Your feet always seem to know the right moves
And ur body always show us you got the best groves
You see
Backn the day
I use to be you
Git up n git movn to the
One step
Makes ur body move to the
Two step
Watch ur feet grove to the

Three step
And you go round N round
Yeah, that waZ the ShiZ nitZ
BackN the day
It was Ah'ight
BackN the day

BackN the Day

The Blog

Don't be afraid
Share it
Don't be afraid
Post it
Don't be afraid to write what's really on your mind
It's a proven fact that we have always been fascinated
By trying to figure out what's on
Someone else's mind
Be diligent with your task
No dirty language I should ask
When you run out of paper or you run out of ink
When your typewriter skips or your computer
Is on the blink
Whether your voice is frail or you have an ingrown
Toe nail
When there's no other way to log it
"Just blog it"

Daybreak

Time heals all wounds
A heart broken knows no way
Laughter so far in the distance
Sorrow befriends when crying begins
A fresh day is on the horizon
Eyes light up from the reflection of the light source
Day breaks forth and the heart is lifted
For the moment

Extinction

So rare
So sweet
Like an angel
Many search for you
Yet find you not
Silently you fly, so high, so low
As a soft breeze gently blow
Through the air quietly you flow
I long for a glimpse of you
In a word
Beautiful
In a thought
Wonderful
In my heart so warm and
As you should be
So free
You're never hiding in your own eyes
Yet abiding where you lay
Bird of paradise
Home
Is where you are

Me the Piano Keys and You

I'm sitting here writing my lyrics on my own
Wondering if I could reach
Wondering if I would reach
That certain one
Who stands alone
Watching
And waiting
For someone like me
I've got to see you
So you can hear me
The words that I make
Here on my knees I beg
Being inspired by
The memories
That toil in my mind
It's time
For the piano
To loosen the keys
That stimulates this erection of love

We belong together
Me
The piano keys
And you

I've been dreaming of you singing
The keys playing
And me saying and saying

I will listen this time
For the cords
That touches upon my
Willowed heart of affection

Soothing and soft to the ear that hears
The last bass lines
That vibrates off the drummers drum
And brings a close
To the running of the keys

It's in the end
That we stand together
In this
The silent bow of humility

Quenched

A dieing soul never thirst for love
A thirsty soul never loves to die
A love that dies never thirst again
A thirsty love never dies
If you thirst for love
Love will die for you
If you die for love
Your thirst will have finally been quenched
Always Love Satisfied
And never become thirsty for anything
But God and water

A Nighttime Prayer

The night was still and the air was crisp
I lay quietly in the bed
At every creek and every crack I clung tighter
To the covers which hid me from the darkness
All around me
With my head beneath the pillow, I could feel
The heat of my breathe as the tears of sweat ran
Down my hidden head beneath my - now wet pillow
My eyes I closed tight and tighter
My body shook from uncontrollable shivers
If only I were asleep was my thought
This was the night time seemed to stand still
In the mist of the terror I remembered a prayer
Then silently, I begun to say
Lord, keep me safe throughout the night
Let me not fear in the mist of this fright
Make me calm and bring light to this gloom
Just then the lights came on as I heard two steps
Wouldn't you know it, mom entered the room

She uncovered my head and wiped the sweat
From my face
She bowed down beside me and kissed so
Softly
With soothing words she said
It's going to be alright
And the night's fears were chased away as she sung
My favorite sweet lullaby
Goodnight

Day Rising

Through the windows the new sun comes a
Glistening
The sparkling wood floor reveals her shine
Fresh scented daisies reflect their color all
Around
With hardly a movement in sight and barely
Even a sound
Dawn has risen and brought us a new day

Perfect Array

Open windows allow fresher air
A room neat and tidy
A fresh scented vacuum
Sheets tucked tightly
Shoes lined against the wall

Classic Melody

Symphonic notes creates a classy rhythm
Harmonic sounds of the woodwinds notes
Drummers drum sets the pace
Brassy brasses creates the melody
The directors' bow signals the end

Eternity

Through the darkness reins much light
The light of the world breaks through the sky
The sky reveals the passage home
Home is where the heart is
Heart is where your treasure lies

Forgiveness Medicine

Hurt and pain enters the scene
No feelings inside to let is show
Tears and crying breaks through the shield
Loneliness and depression wait their turn
Letting it go from the heart brings healing all over

Winds

The winter winds blowing soft and cool add a touch
Of flavor to the air
My lips do quiver and my teeth do chatter
The steps I take are that of a much quickened pace
I find myself in a race against the wind
Trying to hide myself before the naked winds
Pierce through the linings that yet cling to
And cover my body

Indecisive

If you always stand and watch injustice
Who will fight for liberty?
If you always stand and watch partiality
Who will fight for equality?
When a white man loves a black woman or
When an older woman loves a younger man
I ask
Is this perversion, lust or love?
Selah,
Decisions
You hate the right to bear arms
But it is the bullet that mortifies the body
Kill the beast or
Let him live to kill
Love all or hate all
Don't just stand
For neither

Best Friends Forever

Birth brings new life with legs of four
Brown, tan and white fur covers the floor
Whinny yelps heard through the starry night
Cuddles brings calm and builds a lasting bond
Friendship comes in many forms, even mans best

Line Poems to Live By

Overcome every obstacle
So you can always have a reason never to go
Backwards

Always look destiny in the face
So when others look at you
They will see the reflection of it in your eyes

Always count the number of times you fail
So that it will be a testament to how high you
Have climbed when you succeed

Never giving up on yourself
Means to always believe and to always try again

Tired is only tired when you give up and quit

The finish line is only the starting point for a winner

When you reach the end of a good book
Always recommend it to a friend

About The Author

John Simmons Jr., one of six children, born in Hammond, Indiana. Graduated from Hammond High School and from there attended Purdue University and an undergraduate School where he obtained degrees for Computer Technology and an MBA.

He first fell in love with writing in the seventh grade. Since then he has been pursuing his passion for writing. He left the corporate world making over six figures a year to pursue his love of writing full-time. He dedicates time internationally over the Internet and to communities all over by traveling around teaching, coaching, and inspiring everyone with his love for poetry and writing. He is a regular at hosting Open-Mic poetry night readings at business venues, centers and other locations. He has already touched thousands of lives and has founded "The I.C.P.A.", a non-profit organization which helps people explore, embrace, understand and pursue their love of the arts. For more information please visit http://www.theicpa.com/. Many fans and poets know him by his poet name of "quah." He can be booked for Inspirational speaking engagements, poetry readings, featured spoken word artist, storytime reading for kids and more by emailing him at jsimjr@johnsimmonsjr.com or visiting the website http://www.johnsimmonsjr.com/. John also regularly attends Dominion Christian Center in Rockford, IL and loves the Lord God with all his heart, body and soul.

Thank you and may God bless.

Printed in the United States
94841LV00004B/7-54/A

9 781425 978754